WE WILL REMEMBER THEM

We Will Remember Them

by

Gavin Dickson
with D.J. Carswell

10 Publishing
a division of 10 of those.com

First published in Great Britain in 2018

British Library Cataloguing in Publication Data
A record for this book is available from the British Library

ISBN: 978-1-912373-39-0

Cover design by Pete Barnsley (CreativeHoot.com)

10Publishing, a division of 10ofthose.com
Unit C, Tomlinson Road, Leyland, PR25 2DY, England
Email: info@10ofthose.com
Website: www.10ofthose.com

We Will Remember Them

The eleventh hour of the eleventh day of the eleventh month marks the coming into force of the armistice which signalled the end of World War One. At 11 a.m. on 11 November 1918 the guns fell silent after more than four years of continuous, aggressive warfare.

Armistice Day, now known as Remembrance Day, is set aside for us to remember those who gave their lives in both World Wars, as well as the many others who have died in conflicts since 1945. Tragically, most of the names still being added to war memorials throughout the UK are those who sacrificed their lives while only young. Many, many others have survived but carry with them terrible injuries and scars, both physical and mental. To be silent to remember them all for only two minutes in the course of a year seems too little in the light of such overwhelming sacrifice.

We Will Remember Them

On Remembrance Day we reflect as we recite words from the poem 'For the Fallen', written by Laurence Binyon:

They shall not grow old,
As we that are left grow old:
Age shall not weary them,
Nor the years condemn.
At the going down of the sun
And in the morning
We will remember them.[1]

What emotions of gratitude and grief, pride and perplexity, submission and sorrow fill our minds in the quiet moments of meditation, especially as memories of loved ones are stirred.

Flanders, the western part of Belgium, was the scene of some of the most concentrated fighting in World War One. When there was utter devastation of buildings, roads and trees, only the poppy survived. John McCrae, a doctor serving with the Canadian Armed Forces, was so moved by what he saw that, in 1915, he scribbled in his pocket notebook the following poem:

'In Flanders Fields'
In Flanders fields the poppies blow
Between the crosses, row on row,
That mark our place; and in the sky
The larks, still bravely singing, fly
Scarce heard amid the guns below.

We are the Dead. Short days ago
We lived, felt dawn, saw sunset glow,
Loved and were loved, and now we lie
In Flanders fields.

Take up our quarrel with the foe:
To you from failing hands we throw
The torch; be yours to hold it high.
If ye break faith with us who die
We shall not sleep, though poppies grow
In Flanders fields.[2]

Later that year the poem was published by *Punch* magazine, and so the poppy became the symbol of soldiers who died in battle.

Individual battles during World War One conjure up particular details in our minds. With the Battle of the Somme, you think of over-the-top charges and thousands of British soldiers mown down by German machine guns. With Passchendaele, you think of carnage and mud. Just over 100 years have elapsed since that campaign ended in ignominious abandonment, but the images have entered our collective psyche and are still with us today.

It is well known that it rained, and that it rained hard. In fact, the rainfall in low-lying Belgium in August 1917 was the worst that they had experienced for thirty years.Living and fighting in these conditions are far removed from those of modern warfare; we struggle to imagine what it must have been like.[3]

While today's battlefields look very different from those of a century ago, the challenges and sacrifices continue. We need to remember those who have fallen, as well as those affected by the traumas of war.

As we stand and remember each year, what can we say? Is there any hope for our world? When will we call 'time' on these wars and bloody battles? Can peace ever be brokered in our world? In the battles of our personal lives?

What follows is the true story of former Scots Guardsman Gavin Dickson (First Battalion Scots Guards, 2000–2013). He recalls his life as a serving soldier in the British Army but honestly shares how he has found lasting peace amid the challenges and mess of everyday life ...

A Soldier's Story – ASR Gavin Dickson

My cousin Adrian was in the Royal Signals. Every time he came home, he would tell us many stories of his life in the forces. My uncle was based in Germany too. Many recruits come from a military background, so it was not unusual for me to want to follow in my family's footsteps. At the age of sixteen I probably could have joined any regiment but I chose the Scots Guards, which is an infantry unit.

However, I was very small for my age and had been bullied for it at school. I was only eight stone with a small frame. When I had my army daysack on my back, the straps would fall off because my shoulders were so slight!

I would say that when I enlisted I was smart but didn't have much common sense. It took me a long time to gain some traction in the military.

The early days of my military career could be described as my not really knowing much nor grasping what I was supposed to be doing. Most of my peers who joined at the same time were in the same boat as me. Being young, the majority of us didn't progress up the ranks into leadership roles as much as we should have.

My training commenced at Glencorse in Penicuik, Scotland on the junior leadership programme, which lasted six months. After that I was posted to Catterick, North Yorkshire for Phase 2 at the Infantry Training Centre. Then I headed down south to London, where I was to experience my first taste of the 'real' army as a Queen's Guardsman with F Company in the First Battalion Scots Guards. As this is the ceremonial company, it involved donning their bright red uniform and wearing their furry hat![4]

I was in London for about three years. At first this was with F Company in Chelsea Barracks, which was demolished on 26 September 2008 after the site was sold for a housing development. I then moved to C Company as a rifleman. We were based at Wellington Barracks in Birdcage Walk, which is right beside Buckingham Palace, and the battalion took its turn guarding the palace. We also took part in leading the Queen's birthday parade: Trooping the Colour. When we were not guarding the Queen, we did a lot of military exercises, training to be ready for war or any other event that needed military intervention.

One such intervention came during the Fire Brigade strikes in 2002 and 2003; we became temporary firefighters. It was an interesting time, to say the least! Once my friend Kenny and I were getting a hose out. I would usually be the standpipe man responsible for turning the water on and then I would join the others extending the rest of the hose. That day Kenny and I were putting on the very thin nozzle together. But with both of us being slightly built, and the water pressure being so great, we were blown back into a greenhouse, smashing all the glass, which then fell on top of us!

We did a lot of good in this temporary role and we travelled all around London as well. However, the Fire Brigade strikes stopped my regiment going on an important training exercise in Kenya. This in turn stopped my regiment from being available for the Iraq invasion. Having said that, I would have two operational tours of Iraq: Telic 5 in 2005 and Telic 7 in 2007.

Salisbury Plain was one of the places where we did lots of exercises and military manoeuvres. During my first military exercise with F Company, I very quickly found myself involved with signals, using and carrying radio equipment. I also did a similar role in Sennybridge (the third largest military training area in the UK, which lies to the north of the Brecon Beacons National Park in Wales). I had quite an affinity with radio communications, which I maintained all through my army career, whether in a fighting platoon, in the Signals or in the Operations Room in Battalion Headquarters.

Having been based in London, we were then moved to Europe, where we spent six years in Munster, Germany. During that time, we left the role of light infantry and went into armoured infantry, in particular using the Warrior vehicles. These are tracked infantry fighting vehicles – ones that move on caterpillar treads across rough terrain. The Warrior is armed with a 30mm Rarden L21A1 cannon and a 7.62mm chain gun, as well as having a turret that can traverse 360 degrees.[5] I enjoyed this period very much – it was the most stable time I experienced.

Personal battles

Regretfully, I was never the most moral of people. When I got to Germany, I would visit what Germans called 'nightclubs', but what we might recognise as whorehouses, to use prostitutes. I was also known as the man to go and see if you wanted pornography. I had quite a lot of it – a cupboard full of the stuff. This was a good number of years ago, so there wasn't so much of the easy access that the Internet provides today. Men would come to me to borrow the literature I had stashed away.

Men and alcohol are also never far away from each other. Looking back I would describe myself as 'alcohol dependent'. It was not unusual for me to be found in the gutter, totally inebriated. One time, after a very heavy night of drinking, I got into a taxi and was delivered to the wrong camp in Germany! Instead of trying to find my way around, I just slept on the pavement. The next morning was very 'interesting' as, having been delivered back to my camp, I then had to face the Regimental Sergeant Major. I had been lifted from my bed and put into, or rather poured into, my uniform, shaved and then posted at his door, where he tore me apart by shouting very loudly at me for several minutes. It was very uncomfortable, but totally deserved.

I was not the worst kind of guy in the world; I was not the best sort of person either. While not religious, I thought of myself as 'good' and did not really see myself as a 'sinner'. Like many of the young soldiers who join the army, my home life was not straightforward: I can't say that I was raised in a very happy home. When I was a small child, my dad was violent towards my mother, which I witnessed several times. My mum and dad divorced when I was aged about eight. After that most contact with my father was severed until my late teens when I resumed contact with him. This was followed by another lapse in communication until a few years ago. It is only recently that I have felt the beginnings of a relationship with him, both of us being different people from those violent home days.

When I was twelve, my mother met and married my stepdad. With her I grew up in a non-religious home but my mother was very superstitious. She would visit gypsy tents and take part in tarot card readings. Later on in life she loved to watch programmes such as *My Big Fat Gypsy Wedding*. She would want to emulate what she saw, even though this travellers' way of life is not in our DNA. It seemed she was drawn to that culture, with its big dresses and superstition, as well as being attracted to occult practices such as psychics, Ouija boards and the like.

My mother tried very hard to give us a 'good life' as she saw it, and even more so during those years as a single mother. She would work all the hours she could to provide me and my sister with lots of stuff. However, with my mother working so hard, my sister and I were often left to ourselves. I would get up at 6 a.m., then wake my sister at 8 a.m. to get her up before going to primary school. After work, my mother was often extremely tired. She became unwell, being diagnosed after many years with an auto-immune disease called Behcet's, which is a rare disorder that causes blood vessel inflammation throughout your body.

Both my mother and stepdad worked very hard in their jobs and were able to buy their home – initially the council house I was raised in. My stepdad was a very warm man but he would do anything for an easy Iife – he was very agreeable towards my mother but Mum ruled the roost.

Iraq to Canada

My company continued in Germany for six years, doing the kind of roles that required armoured infantry work, including two tours of Iraq. My first tour was interesting – a few rockets were fired at us and there was one notable small-arms contact – but generally it was quiet. This was in 2005, during Operation Telic 5, when the warfare had ended and everything seemed to be going quite well. The university was open and by then boys and girls were going back to school. There is a picture of me in the *Scots Guards Magazine* playing football with a lot of young Iraqi boys. I have my body armour on but am wearing my beret, my soft hat.

However, when we returned in 2007 for Telic 7, everything had changed. The university was still open but the schools had closed. The mullahs and religious factions had come back into power and back into the political arena. An insurgency had also been raging throughout the country. So we had to exchange our berets for helmets and full body armour. In fact, you didn't travel unless you were in an armoured vehicle. In 2005 we had moved around by driving in snatch wagons or cut-down Land Rovers, which were very exposed to the elements, especially the wind. Yet in 2007 we moved around in the Warrior, a 26-ton armoured fighting vehicle.

The full force of the insurgents was felt by their use of IEDs (improvised explosive devices). We had seen several IED strikes. However, our tour was in winter so it was still quite quiet. In most of the Arab world, but especially in Iraq and Afghanistan, when the weather becomes colder, the fighting generally starts to decrease. As the temperature goes up again, though, so does the level of fighting. Despite the relative quiet of both our tours of Iraq, we were surrounded by death, with the death of Guardsman Ray during pre-deployment training, two deaths caused by car accidents while on leave in the UK, and the operational death of Guardsman Stephen Ferguson, known as Fergie. (Fergie's Warrior slid into a canal while on patrol in Basra. Though his team got him out, it was too late.) Despite these events, though, I was not really thinking about what would have happened to me if I had died.

From our German base we were posted back to Catterick Garrison, in the UK. This garrison is blessed with a large training area perfect for infantry training with its hard terrain, steep hills, forested areas and large open grass areas. Beyond it being ideal for training, it is very beautiful. From there, in our role as armoured infantry, we travelled to Canada, where we spent six months. For two months we did what we call 'activations': getting the vehicles ready for the battalion training. From that I then moved to being part of the safety staff. In this role I was part of a team that made sure everyone was shooting in the right direction and was safe. Then it was time for me and my company to be tested.

This final training test in Canada assesses whether the battalion is fit for deployment on live operations or not. There are many different training scenarios given. Everyone must use the full range of weapons in a safe and right manner, and all your vehicles must be passed as safe. Lastly, there is a dry training exercise during which blank rounds are fired. At our testing, as is always the case, the Scots Guards including my own company were given the 'green light', achieving a grade 6, which is the highest grade a battalion can achieve.

Free coffee

It was during this time that I met a young lady called Alison and we began to date. Like many other lads, I brought Alison back to live with me – in Lanark, where I had a house.

Having settled in to life together, we were looking for some social things to do in and around our town. One day, in the library, Alison came across a little leaflet advertising an event with free Starbucks coffee. We didn't have a Starbucks locally; it sounded good to us. What we hadn't realised was that it was being organised by a church! Nevertheless, we went along. I drank the coffee and Alison looked at the displays.

Now you will have guessed that church and God didn't exactly figure in my life. The odd instances that faith or the Bible crossed my mind were rare. As a child I sometimes attended the Christmas Eve service with my family or just with my mother, but it was only for show and often we would leave early. My next-door neighbours, two doors down, did go to church on Sundays. One summer I remember going to Sunday school with their children for a six-week period, and I enjoyed it. Another time, when I was twelve, me and my friend Gary had our blades on and were skating past the chapel. It was a Sunday and nearly one o'clock. We thought that there was a wedding or some function on there as the young priest invited us in for a drink of juice and biscuits, and had a bit of a chat with us. Gary and I went again after a couple of weeks, but not much after that.

As a young soldier there were other occasions when I had some religious experience. When I was about sixteen or seventeen and in London, I would often go down to St Paul's Cathedral just to sit there. It gave me a real sense of peace, but inside my heart I was a very angry young man. *Very* angry. The sort of things I had witnessed from my father as a child had hurt me emotionally quite a bit. I wasn't speaking to him and wanted revenge.

Then, during my training to go to Iraq, I heard that a colleague of mine, David Craig, had died. A Warrior armoured vehicle had reversed over him, killing him. At first we had to carry on with the exercise because we were preparing to go on tour – apart from David's crew and vehicle, which were separated while there was an investigation into what had happened. Afterwards, though, we went to what we call a cookhouse or 'scoff hall' where we held a service for David. As the pipes and drums played the well-known hymn 'Amazing Grace', I remember being really touched by the sound of this and the words.

I had very little to do with God, faith and the Bible. When Alison picked up that little leaflet offering free coffee at a local church, it was surprising we both decided to go along. Even more unexpectedly, we continued to attend the church each Sunday. That was possible as I was based at Catterick while my battalion was preparing to go to Afghanistan, so I was allowed home to Lanark at the weekends.

We liked the people we met there, including the pastor, Michael, and his wife, Esther. While I didn't go along with everything they did, basically they were very genuine people who loved Jesus and who sought to tell and teach others about Him. Each time we met, I would ask Michael difficult questions: Why is there suffering in the world? Who is Jesus? Why did He come into the world?

All this led on to Michael teaching me from the Bible the simple basics of the gospel. Everyone has done wrong (I couldn't argue with that when I thought about it) and that wrong, or sin, has cut us off from God. God is just and must punish wrongdoing. But God is also loving and loves us so much that He sent His son Jesus to die on the cross in order to take this punishment in our place. Then, on that first Easter morning, Jesus rose victorious from the dead. He is alive and has gone to prepare a place in heaven for all those who have asked Him for forgiveness, trusting Him as their Saviour and Rescuer. This is what Easter is all about! Esther explained this very clearly one day, saying, 'You are a sinner and you need to ask God to forgive you. Come to Him, repent and be saved!'

I joined in with the refreshments after that church service but straightaway had to leave to get back in time to the garrison at Catterick. It is a long drive so I had plenty of time to think about what I had heard. Just around Penrith, I turned the radio off, though I continued driving. Not being what you might call an expert in prayer, I prayed as simply and as best as I could: 'If this dude (meaning Jesus!) really did these things for me, then I need to know Him.' Although I maybe didn't know the right words to say, I was being genuine and God knew that.

Wonderfully and miraculously I knew at that moment I had become a Christian. I was truly sorry for my rotten sin. God sent His Holy Spirit to dwell within me, and my heart, the real me, was changed. This new relationship with God was so real. Now, of course, I know verses from the Bible that explain all this, but that night in my car in the North of England was when God saved me and became real to me.

The following weekend Gavin went with the battalion to Wales. But although outwardly in his uniform he looked the same, inwardly something radical had happened:

I knew God. I had this great hunger to read the Bible – I couldn't put it down. Every day was an opportunity to discover more about Jesus. My friends were shocked, asking, 'What has happened to Dicko [their nickname for me]?' Of course, I realised quickly that how I had been living was not right. Alison had returned to Canada before I came to faith. (We had found the process of getting her a visa difficult, but anyway she realised she wanted to have a more carefree attitude to life rather than settling down with responsibilities.) Now the pornography went. Ended too was my going out at night and having copious amounts to drink. Instead, in came my increasing desire to read, on my own, and wanting to read, of all things, the Bible! My taste in music had also altered somewhat – it became more common for me to be listening to modern music with Christian lyrics. My friends probably thought that I had gone mad. They all, including my best friend, took the change they saw in me quite badly.

Things like pornography and drunkenness were not considered to be wrong by those around me. But I began to see things from God's perspective. After all that He had done for me – He who is so pure and holy that He can't even look at sin – *still* He loves me. So how could I carry on doing things that caused Him so much pain? My world was turned not only upside down but right way up … and in front of a barrack full of lads.

However, it took me a while to stop drinking at the levels I was used to. I had become alcohol dependent, which, apart from anything else, was very bad for my health long term. My relationship with God also, naturally, took time to develop. At school, having been only taught that we came about by evolution, I had never questioned how or why we are here on earth. But as I began to understand about God, and what He has done as the Creator, slowly my relationship with God as my Heavenly Father deepened. Many soldiers have not had good experiences of earthly fathers. So it was an eye-opening and heart-warming experience to come to know God personally as the one true God and Father of humankind.

Another area of my life that dramatically changed was my language. Michael, the pastor, has always been very patient with me, especially over the matter of my foul mouth. When I first met him in church, I refused to stop swearing! I reasoned, 'I am a soldier and that is what soldiers do!' Michael never reacted badly to such comments but was always gracious and kind. Something happened, however, that day on the A66 when I prayed to God for the first time. Something 'clicked' and from then on I stopped swearing. To this day I struggle to swear –

something stops me, even if I want to. Even if I am in a bad place and feel I want to swear, it doesn't come out but gets stuck. It is like a mental block – a block I believe God has put in place. God has done something *for* me and *to* me. He has not only cleaned up my foul heart but also given me a clean mouth.

Of course, not everything in my life was sorted out straight away. I had (and still have) a lot to learn with God's help.

Afghanistan

It was early January 2010 when we left a cold, snowy Catterick garrison for our tour to Afghanistan. My home church family was very supportive, trying to encourage me as a new Christian and as a soldier going to a battlefield. Before I left, they shared this Bible verse with me: 'Your word is a lamp for my feet, a light on my path' (Psalm 119:105).

Later, I was walking down the path beside a snow-covered road. The light from the cars around was reflecting off the snow under my feet, creating little pools of light that reminded me of Psalm 119. That moment really impacted me. It brought to mind those words of Scripture: that God was with me and would indeed guide my path as I set off for Afghanistan. I did not take this to be a promise that God was *not* going to let me die, but that God's Word, the Bible, would continue to show me the right way to follow God wherever I might be.

As Right Flank of the Scots Guards (Armoured Infantry Company), we deployed three months ahead of the main battalion and joined Operation Herrick, the code name used for all British operations in Afghanistan from 2002 to 2014. Our job was to patrol in the Warriors. These fighting vehicle were considered a genuine asset for pretty much the whole of the British operation in the rough terrain of Afghanistan.

All the way through the tour, I tried to be the lead person or in the lead vehicle because I knew, from God's Word, where I was going if I died. Because of that day when I trusted Jesus Christ as my personal Saviour, I knew that I had been saved. So when my life on this earth ends, in whatever way, I am sure that I will go straight to be with God in heaven. However, most of my team, platoon and company didn't know who Jesus is. I was ready to die but I knew that many others were unprepared.

The Ministry of Defence describes the company as having experienced considerable success during its involvement in Operation Herrick. Tragically however, there were fatalities and injuries sustained. Fellow comrades found those times of loss extremely tough and a blow to morale. This is when and where all that vigorous training, which has been carefully planned and carried out, comes into its own.

A colleague of Gavin called Lance Sergeant David Walker was fatally wounded by insurgent fire in February 2010, while conducting a ground domination patrol. He was employed as a Section Commander within Right Flank, which had been playing a vital part in Operation Moshtarak since the beginning of the month. David was responsible for commanding and leading a four-man fire team that was tasked with reassuring the local population as well as defeating the insurgents.

Gavin remembers:

It was a big blow losing David Walker; dealing with that was quite tough. Then I saw my friend Jack get injured when his Warrior struck a very large IED. Jack lost his spleen and suffered multiple injuries. Usually I tried to be in the lead vehicle so it should have been me at the front. But that day I was involved in a supply drop, so his vehicle jumped ahead of ours – and was struck. As the driver of our Warrior, I had to be ready to move to provide engine revs for the chain gun to work. I could not get out to assess the situation. It was very hard being stuck in my vehicle – so *very* hard. (Since then, though, Jack has recovered quite well from his injuries – he's not too bad now.)

The day after Jack's injuries happened, I wrote a letter to my home church, asking them to pray for us – which they did – as I felt very much broken inside. I had a lot of misplaced guilt seeing Jack injured in the place where I should have been. Thankfully a lovely padre, Rev. Dr Simon Bloxham-Rose, whom I had bumped into a few days before at the brew area in the Lancaster Regiment's Camp, came especially to chat with us and see how we were – he suddenly appeared, jumping off a helicopter. Looking back, I believe it was God who had sent him at the right time. The padre brought great comfort to me through his ministry and care for us. In fact, every time I went into a new camp, I would meet a padre who sustained me in my faith.

Meanwhile, our company was given a different role and launched out on vehicle patrols. The rest of the battalion came out in the middle of our tour, so we slowly got absorbed back into the battalion as a brigade asset. When the Scots Guards came out, we moved to a new location. Having done the job they were made for, the Warriors were packed up for the remainder of the tour. Our workload changed and involved taking command of small compounds and holding our ground, and not doing much vehicle patrolling. The rest of the tour for us was a low-key affair and relatively uneventful.

However, in July 2010 we heard of the death of Lance Corporal Stephen Monkhouse, who was known and loved by all. Affectionately nicknamed 'Monkey', he was a very tall guy with an ever-present smile. He and Yorkshireman Corporal Matthew Stenton were killed when members of the Royal Dragoon Guards and First Battalion Scots Guards were providing security for the building of Route Trident in Basharan, north of Lashkar Gah. Matthew was commanding a Viking armoured vehicle – which was part of a cordon to facilitate the removal of IEDs – and Monkey was the gunner of a Coyote vehicle when insurgents shot and wounded a member of ISAF (the International Security Assistance Force). Matthew manoeuvred his vehicle in order to lay down fire support and facilitate the evacuation of the casualty. Tragically, as the evacuation was being carried out, Matthew and Monkey were both killed by small-arms fire.

As Lieutenant Colonel Lincoln Jopp, Commanding Officer of First Battalion Scots Guards, said: 'Monkey died coming to the aid of a guardsman who had been shot. He did what every soldier hopes he will have the courage to do if the need arises: he laid down his life for his friend. We salute him and we honour our fallen.' Monkey was awarded, posthumously, the Military Cross.

His death affected quite a few people, including myself and Lance Corporal Michael Little. He took me aside to talk inside the Warrior about the loss of Monkey. The battalion had been hit and had suffered several casualties, including three or four triple amputees, after hitting IEDs. It was a proper fighting situation; proper warfare. Bad things were happening all around.

It was a very difficult time for me, but through it all I kept praying, talking to God. In my head I would think about the words of 'Blessed be Your Name', a Christian song I liked very much and which summed up my feelings amid my circumstances. The song reminds us that in times of suffering we can still choose to praise God, who gives – and takes away – all things.

SASRA

As you can imagine, after all that Gavin had witnessed – the injuries of others, the fatalities, plus the sheer hard work of the tour – it was no wonder that it took him a little while to settle back home. But at Catterick there was a chef called Kennedy who was well known for his happy temperament and big smile. He even won an award, a Commander's commendation, for being 'happy Kennedy'! Each week, with Kennedy and another soldier called Gareth, Gavin would go to the home of Mark Reynolds, an army Scripture Reader.

Gavin continues his story:

There a group of us – several soldiers from across the garrison and some civilians – would study the Bible, pray and sing some hymns. Mark and his wife were always welcoming and their home was so warm and friendly. The fellowship and Bible study were very important, and remained so for my time in the army.

Quite quickly after Afghanistan I was posted up to Edinburgh as part of the regimental support team, which aimed to recruit for the Scots Guards. There I met another army Scripture Reader, David Murray, whose friendship and mentorship remain very important to me today. Having an open home and inviting soldiers to study the Bible there is an important part of SASRA (the Soldiers' and Airmen's Scripture Readers Association).

Wherever I went in this new posting I would try to meet up with Christians for prayer or to read the Bible. It was very much a training ground for what I do now, working full-time for SASRA with the British Army. I am now married to Pauline, whom I met before leaving the army. With our two sons, Malachi and Harvey, we are currently based in Germany.

Christianity is not about doing our best, or even our duty. Rather it is about us turning from our sinful ways and trusting Jesus to forgive us. He made this possible when He died in our place on the cross. Peace is offered by God, as Jesus takes our sin on Himself.

As the Bible says:

He lifted me out of the slimy pit,
out of the mud and mire;
he set my feet on a rock
and gave me a firm place to stand.
He put a new song in my mouth ... (Psalm 40:2–3)

And:

Greater love has no one than this: to lay down one's life for one's friends (John 15:13).

SASRA

SASRA offers Christian support and friendship for Armed Forces personnel. Their patron is Her Majesty the Queen, and their president is General the Lord Dannatt. The organisation dates back to 1838 when originally their members literally read the Scriptures to servicemen because many were unable to read the Bible for themselves. The title of Scripture Reader has stuck, despite its strangeness to modern ears!

All the Scripture Readers are ex-Service men or women, many having become Christians while serving. Although civilians, they are required to wear uniform for ease of recognition, but carry no rank or privileges. Wherever possible, Scripture Readers and their families live in Service Families Accommodation and their homes are 'open' to all for advice, help and encouragement.

References

1 Laurence Binyon, 'For the Fallen', first published in *The Times* on 21 September 1914.

2 John McCrae, 'In Flanders Fields', first published in *Punch* magazine on 8 December 1915.

3 These two paragraphs are taken from Paul Mackrell, *Evangelical Times*, December 2017. Adapted with permission.

4 The Scots Guards is one of the Foot Guards regiments in the army. Originally part of the personal bodyguard of King Charles I of England and Scotland in the seventeenth century, the regiment claims to have been active since 6 March 1642. It has become one of the toughest fighting units in the British Army, renowned for discipline and courage in battle, and has won an outstanding ninety-three battle honours and eleven Victoria Crosses, fighting in every major conflict with distinction. As a mechanised infantry regiment, it is trained to use speed to cross the battlefield quickly and launch onto difficult objectives.

Besides this challenging role in combat, the general public would be more familiar with their other and more 'glamorous' role, performed by the regiment's ceremonial company: that of acting as guards at royal residences such as Windsor Castle and Buckingham Palace. Photographed by thousands and known all over the world, the guards, resplendent in their bright red tunics and bearskin hats, perform their duties in immaculate style.

5 The crew of a Warrior fighting vehicle comprises the driver, seated in the front hull, and the gunner and commander, who are both seated in the turret. Warrior section vehicles can carry up to nine fully equipped infantry soldiers, who sit facing each other in the rear, together with supplies and weapons for a long battlefield day, even in nuclear, biological or chemical conditions.